Where in the World Can I...

FIND A DINOSAUR?

Where in the World Can I...

FIND A DINOSAUR?

www.worldbook.com

World Book, Inc.
180 North LaSalle Street, Suite 900
Chicago, Illinois 60601
USA

For information about other World Book publications, visit our website at **www.worldbook.com** or call **1-800-WORLDBK (967-5325).**

For information about sales to schools and libraries, call 1-800-975-3250 (United States), or 1-800-837-5365 (Canada).

Library of Congress Cataloging-in-Publication Data for this volume has been applied for.

Where in the World Can I…
ISBN: 978-0-7166-5251-9 (set, hc.)

Find a Dinosaur?
ISBN: 978-0-7166-5253-3 (hc.)
ISBN: 978-0-7166-5265-6 (pf.)

Also available as:
ISBN: 978-0-7166-5259-5 (e-book)

STAFF

Executive Committee
President
  Geoff Broderick

Vice President, Editorial
  Tom Evans

Vice President, Finance
  Donald D. Keller

Vice President, International
  Eddy Kisman

Vice President, Technology
  Jason Dole

Director, Human Resources
  Bev Ecker

Editorial
Senior Editor
  Shawn Brennan

Curriculum Designer
  Caroline Davidson

Proofreader
  Nathalie Strassheim

Graphics and Design
Senior Visual Communications Designer
  Melanie Bender

Coordinator, Design Development and Production
  Brenda Tropinski

Senior Media Editor
  Rosalia Bledsoe

Acknowledgments
Writer: Cynthia O'Brien

Produced by
Focus Strategic Communications Inc.

TABLE OF CONTENTS

WHAT IS A DINOSAUR?

A dinosaur is a prehistoric reptile.
Dinosaurs first appeared over 230 million
years ago, and then *evolved* (changed
over time). The group grew to include
dinosaurs of all different shapes and sizes.
Some dinosaurs were as small as hummingbirds.
Others were giant creatures, many times larger than
today's elephants. Dinosaurs lived all over the world for
about 160 million years. About 66 million years
ago, most dinosaurs became *extinct* (died out).

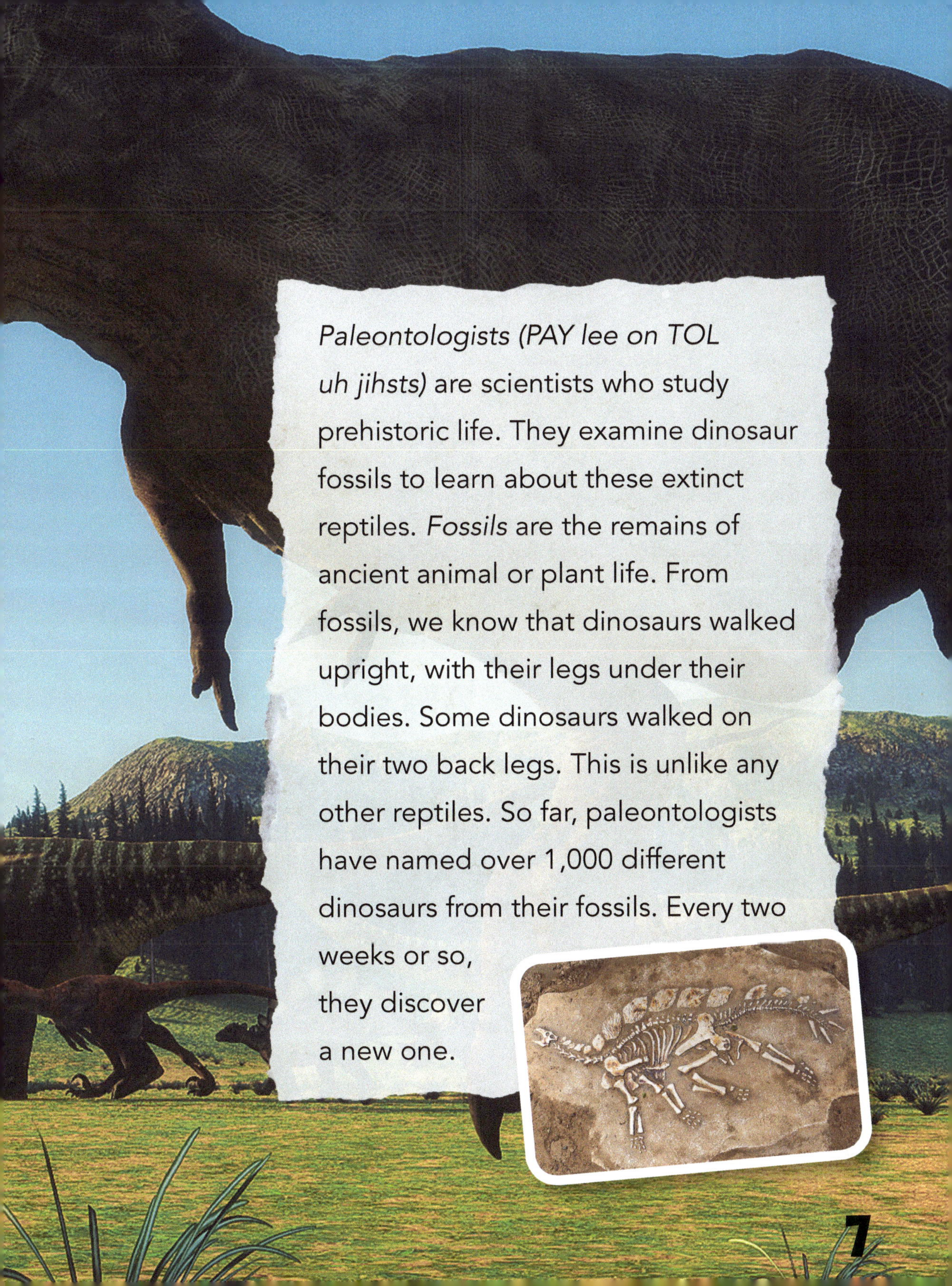

Paleontologists (PAY lee on TOL uh jihsts) are scientists who study prehistoric life. They examine dinosaur fossils to learn about these extinct reptiles. *Fossils* are the remains of ancient animal or plant life. From fossils, we know that dinosaurs walked upright, with their legs under their bodies. Some dinosaurs walked on their two back legs. This is unlike any other reptiles. So far, paleontologists have named over 1,000 different dinosaurs from their fossils. Every two weeks or so, they discover a new one.

Dinosaurs lived in three time periods. They were the Triassic Period (252 million years ago to 201 million years ago), the Jurassic Period (201 million years ago to about 145 million years ago), and the Cretaceous Period (145 million years ago to 66 million years ago).

Scientists divide dinosaurs into two main groups. There are bird-hipped dinosaurs called ornithischians *(awr nuh THIHS kee uhnz)* and lizard-hipped dinosaurs called saurischians *(saw RIHS kee uhnz).*

All ornithischian dinosaurs were plant eaters. *Stegosaurus* first appeared in the Jurassic Period. It had large, bony plates along its back and a powerful, spiked tail. Later, other bird-hipped dinosaurs appeared, including long-necked *Apatosaurus (uh pat oh SAWR uhs)* and horned *Triceratops (try SEHR uh tops)*.

Saurischian dinosaurs included large plant-eating dinosaurs and ferocious meat-eaters called *theropods (THEHR uh pahds)*. *Argentinosaurus (AR gent eenoh SAWR uhs)*, a plant eater, was one of the largest land animals ever. It weighed about 77 tons and was about 130 feet (40 meters) long. *Tyrannosaurus (tih ran uh SAWR uhs)* was a meat-eating predator, or hunter, with a massive head and sharp teeth.

Why did most dinosaurs die out 66 million years ago? Most scientists believe that an asteroid or comet struck Earth. The impact created enormous waves and blasted burning rock around the world. For years, thick dust dimmed the sun. Many animals, including most dinosaurs, could not survive the cooler temperatures.

However, birds did survive. For many years, scientists thought *Archaeopteryx (ahr kee OP tuhr ihks)* was the first true bird. In the 1960's, paleontologists found that *Deinonychus*, a theropod dinosaur, had a birdlike skeleton and feathers. Over thirty years later, scientists in China found *Sinosauropteryx (sine oh sore OP turh ihks)*, another feathered theropod. Many feathered dinosaurs have been found since.

Most scientists now agree that modern birds evolved from these feathered theropods. *Archaeopteryx* was part of this evolution. Over millions of years, smaller, winged birds appeared. When you see a bird today, you are looking at a living dinosaur!

Like you, many people are fascinated by dinosaurs. They have been looking for fossils since the first discoveries in the early 1800's. The name "dinosaur" was first used in 1842. It comes from the word *Dinosauria*, which means "terribly great lizards." We now know that dinosaurs were not lizards at all. They were a different kind of reptile.

Paleontologists have discovered a lot about these special reptiles by studying their fossil remains. They use such technology as CT scanners to study their finds. This is an X-ray computer system that creates images of the inner structure. Technology like this allows paleontologists to reconstruct dinosaur skeletons, learn how these creatures moved, and even find out what they ate.

There are awesome exhibits in parks and museums around the world. Read on to see where you can find dinosaurs up close and in person!

SHANDONG TIANYU NATURE MUSEUM

Since the 1990's, China has become a leader in dinosaur fossil discoveries. You can see some of these amazing finds at Shandong Tianyu Nature Museum. The museum is south of Beijing in Pingyi County, Shandong Province. According to *The Guinness Book of World Records*, the museum is the largest of its kind in the world. When you visit, you can wander through 28 exhibition halls, see over 390,000 exhibits, and watch the prehistoric world in motion at the 3-D cinema.

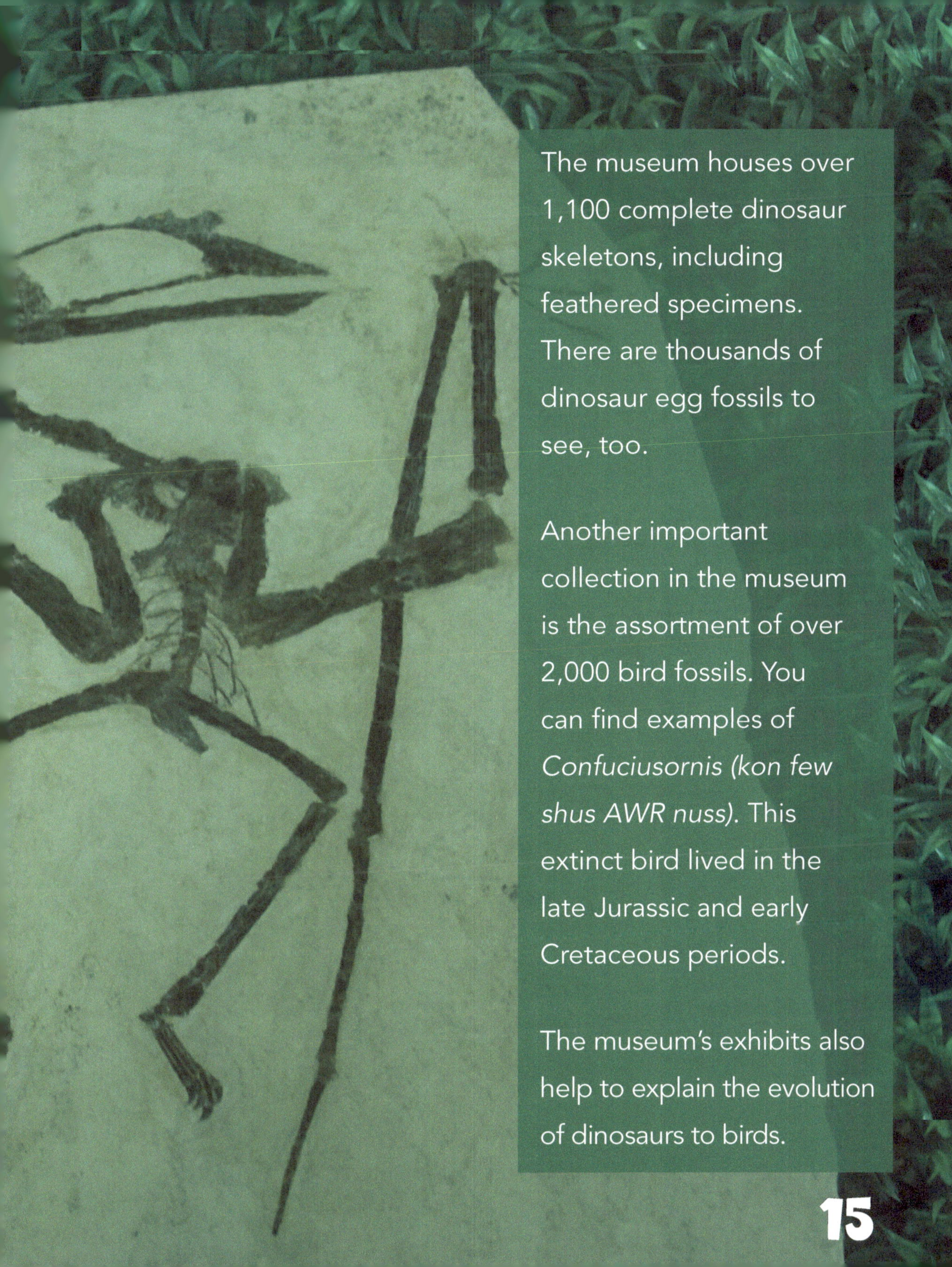

The museum houses over 1,100 complete dinosaur skeletons, including feathered specimens. There are thousands of dinosaur egg fossils to see, too.

Another important collection in the museum is the assortment of over 2,000 bird fossils. You can find examples of *Confuciusornis (kon few shus AWR nuss)*. This extinct bird lived in the late Jurassic and early Cretaceous periods.

The museum's exhibits also help to explain the evolution of dinosaurs to birds.

Dragon Hall holds major dinosaur exhibits. A walk through there takes you past a reconstruction of a massive sauropod called *Mamenchisaurus (mah MEN chi SAWR us)*. Sauropods were long-necked plant eaters. *Mamenchisaurus* had one of the longest necks of all the sauropods.

The *Mamenchisaurus* in Dragon Hall is over 78 feet (24 meters) long from its head to the end of its tail. Many mamenchisaur fossils were found in the Sichuan Basin, in southwest China.

A 26-foot- (8-meter-) long *Iguanodon* (*ih GWAN uh dahn*) is another find in Dragon Hall. *Iguanodon* was a plant eater with strong back legs and shorter arms. It had five fingers on each hand and a sharp spike on each thumb. *Iguanodon* fossils have been found all over the world, except Antarctica.

Since many fossils have been found close together, scientists believe that *Iguanodon* lived in herds.

What other creatures lived among the dinosaurs? Explore the Marine and Insect halls to see fossils of prehistoric fish, other marine life, and insects. Inside Guizhou Hall, there are sea lilies, ammonites, and gastropods on display.

But the highlight of this hall is the ichthyosaur (*IHK thee uh sawr*) fossils. Ichthyosaurs were fishlike reptiles that became extinct about 90 million years ago.

The ones you can find in Guizhou Hall range from very small fossils to large 59-foot (18-meter) specimens.

Moving on to the Hezheng Biota Hall, there are early mammals, such as elephants and a rhinoceros. Many early mammal fossils have been found in Liaoning Province, in northeastern China. Mammal and dinosaur specimens found in Liaoning were buried in volcano ash and well-preserved. Some mammals died out with the dinosaurs. Others evolved into the many large and small species we have today.

The research center is an important part of the Tianyu Nature Museum. Paleontologists who work there study the fossils in the collection as well as new specimens. Since the 1990's, China has been a rich source of dinosaur fossil finds. The microraptor, a small, feathered dinosaur, was discovered in Liaoning Province. These finds helped to make the link between prehistoric dinosaurs and today's birds. You can find some of them at Tianyu and other Chinese museums.

In 2015, paleontologists at the Tianyu Nature Museum reported a rare new discovery. They called the fossil *Yi qi*, which means "strange wing" in the Chinese language, Mandarin. It was the first time that scientists had discovered a dinosaur with batlike wings. It was another link between dinosaurs and birds. *Yi qi* was smaller than a microraptor and probably used its wings to glide through the air.

DINOSAUR NATIONAL MONUMENT

Most museums do not let people touch the exhibits. Things are different at Dinosaur National Monument. Here, you can touch a real dinosaur bone that is 149 million years old! The park spreads across 329 square miles (852 square kilometers) along the Colorado and Utah border in the western United States. Millions of years ago, this part of the United States was home to dinosaurs of the Jurassic and Cretaceous periods.

In 1909, a paleontologist named Earl Douglass explored a rocky area in northeast Utah. This was a section of the Morrison Formation. It is a long stretch of rocks that is between 155 million and 148 million years old. Douglass's first discovery was eight tailbones of an *Apatosaurus*. He found many other fossils in the rocks. In 1915, the United States government created the Dinosaur National Monument to protect the fossil site.

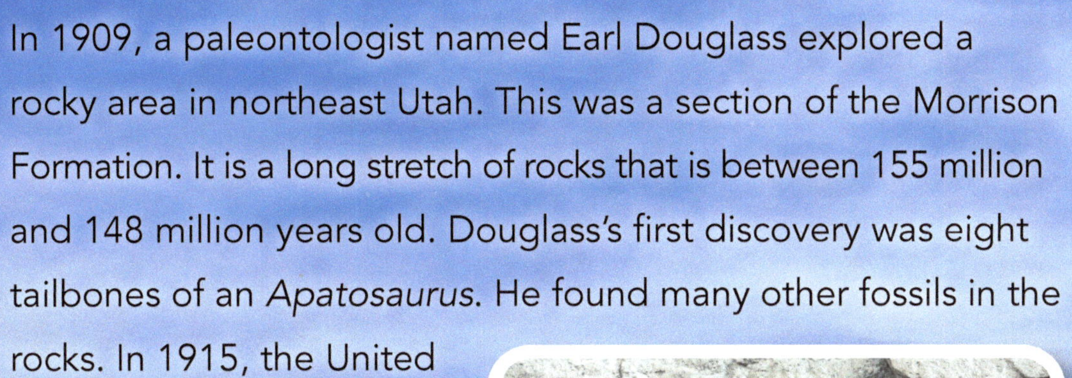

EXIT
Exit Only
Exit Only

Today, you can find Douglass's *Apatosaurus* at the Carnegie
Museum of Natural History, in Pittsburgh, Pennsylvania.
But Douglass continued to work at the site in Utah, which
he called the Carnegie Quarry. Until the 1920's, the museum
in Pittsburgh continued to collect fossils from the quarry.

Many other fossils remained in Utah and became part of the
Dinosaur National Monument. Inside Quarry Exhibit Hall,
you can walk along a long, high wall of rock that contains
about 1,500 bones from different dinosaurs.

The remains are just as they were left millions of years ago.
An ancient river probably carried the bones along and
deposited them. Over time, layers of rock formed over
and around the bones.

Across from the wall, a tall,
reconstructed *Allosaurus*
(al uh SAWR uhs) towers over
visitors. Behind it, a mural
shows how the fierce, meat-eating dinosaur may have
looked when it was alive.

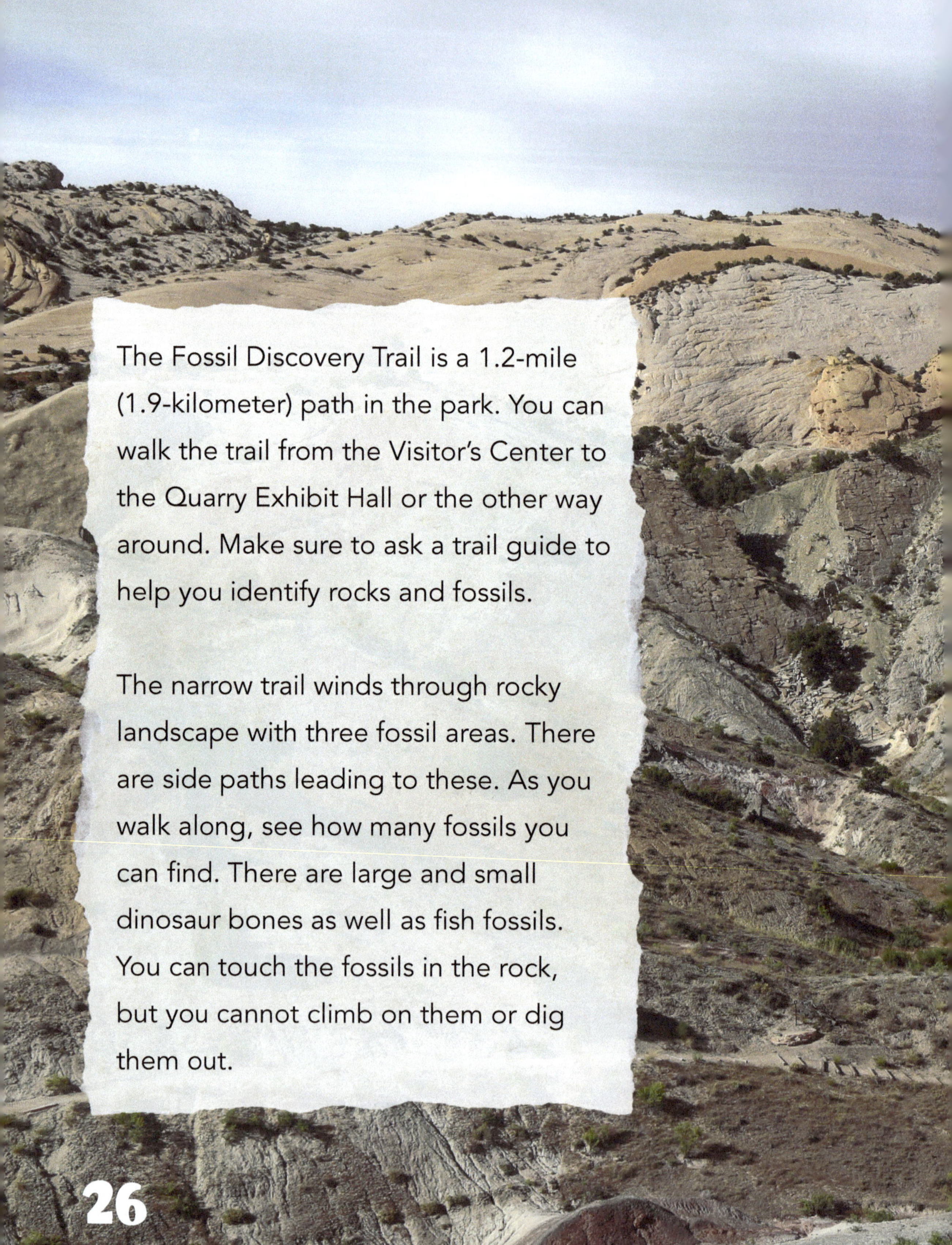

The Fossil Discovery Trail is a 1.2-mile (1.9-kilometer) path in the park. You can walk the trail from the Visitor's Center to the Quarry Exhibit Hall or the other way around. Make sure to ask a trail guide to help you identify rocks and fossils.

The narrow trail winds through rocky landscape with three fossil areas. There are side paths leading to these. As you walk along, see how many fossils you can find. There are large and small dinosaur bones as well as fish fossils. You can touch the fossils in the rock, but you cannot climb on them or dig them out.

At one section of the trail, there are *petroglyphs*. These are rock carvings made by ancient people. There are more petroglyphs to see in other parts of the park.

The landscape of the park looked very different when dinosaurs lived. There were large rivers surrounded by trees, ferns, and other plants.

Many of the dinosaurs found in Dinosaur National Monument were sauropods, such as *Diplodocus (duh PLOD uh kuhs). Diplodocus* was a large dinosaur that grew to about 90 feet (27 meters) long. Other dinosaurs that lived in this area include *Camarasaurus (KAM ar uh SAWR uhs)* and *Stegosaurus.* These plant eaters may have been hunted by meat-eating theropods, such as *Ceratosaurus (SEHR uh toh SAWR uhs). Ceratosaurus* was a fierce predator, about 23 feet (7 meters) long.

Paleontologists continue to uncover new finds at Dinosaur National Monument. Their most recent discoveries include the remains of four plant-eating dinosaurs called *Abydosaurus (uh BUY dough SAWR uhs)*. Often, dinosaur skulls are destroyed or damaged. Two of the *Abydosaurus* skulls are complete.

DINOSAUR PROVINCIAL PARK

You will find spectacular dinosaur remains when you visit Dinosaur Provincial Park in Alberta, in western Canada. The sprawling park is about 147 miles (235 kilometers) southeast of Calgary. In 1979, it became a United Nations Educational, Scientific and Cultural Organization (UNESCO) World Heritage Site.

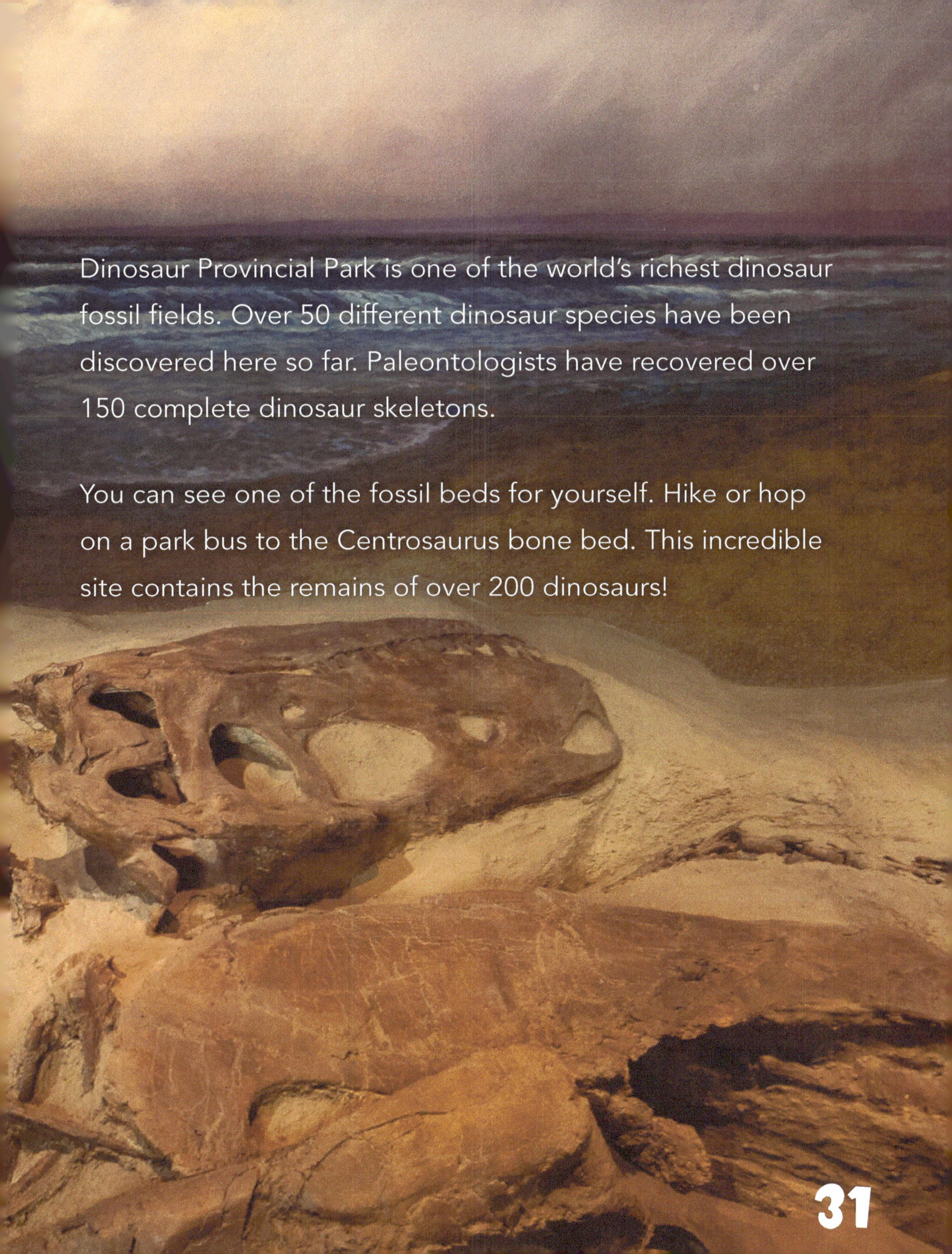

Dinosaur Provincial Park is one of the world's richest dinosaur fossil fields. Over 50 different dinosaur species have been discovered here so far. Paleontologists have recovered over 150 complete dinosaur skeletons.

You can see one of the fossil beds for yourself. Hike or hop on a park bus to the Centrosaurus bone bed. This incredible site contains the remains of over 200 dinosaurs!

Dinosaur Provincial Park spreads over some of Alberta's *badlands*. Millions of years ago, rivers flowed through the area and left deposits. This created the landscape we see today. It is mostly dry land of hills, valleys, and strange rock formations called *hoodoos*.

During the Cretaceous Period, this part of Alberta was filled with subtropical forests, rivers, and an inland sea. The warm weather and lush plant life was an ideal environment for such dinosaurs as *Lambeosaurus (lam BEE oh SAWR uhs)* to thrive.

ROYAL TYRRELL
MUSEUM

After seeing the fossils at Dinosaur
Provincial Park, the next stop is the
Royal Tyrrell Museum. The museum
is near Drumheller, Alberta, about
100 miles (160 kilometers) northwest
of the park. Here you will find one
of the world's largest and most
spectacular collections of dinosaurs.

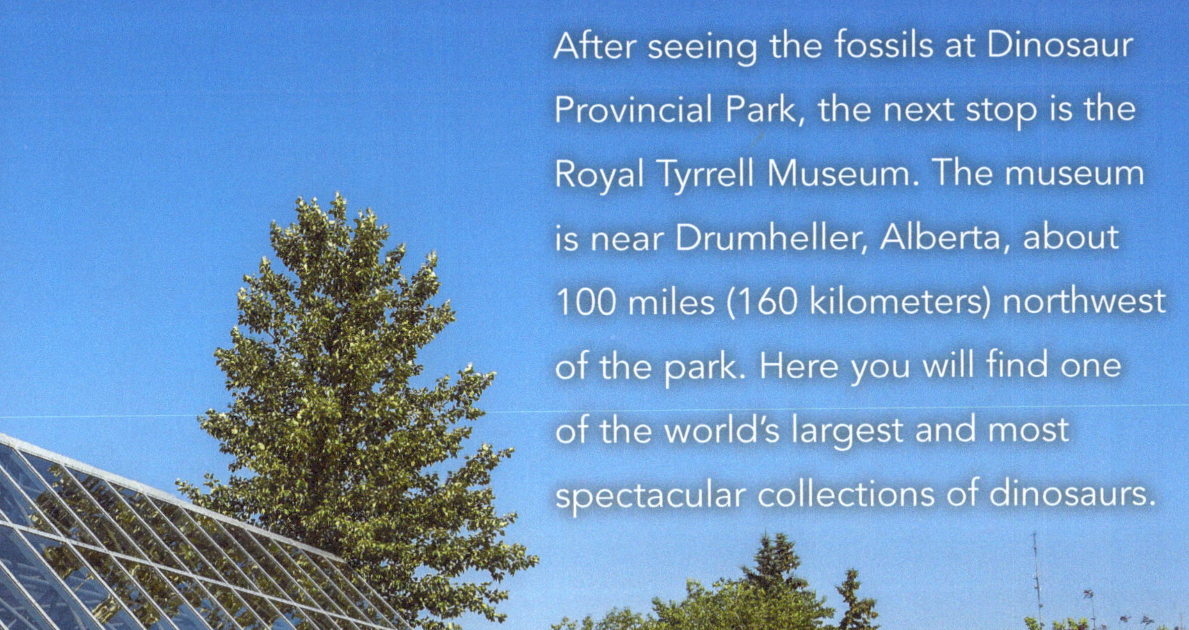

Dinosaur Hall has more than 40 dinosaur displays.
You can stare up at massive skeletons of *Triceratops*
and *Tyrannosaurus rex*. In the Preparation Lab, you
can even see paleontologists at work preparing
fossils to investigate.

DIGGING UP DINOS

To find fossils, scientists often look in places with very old rock. They use satellite images (taken from space) to see large areas of Earth's surface. This helps them to identify the type of rock in an area. Paleontologists also search sites where dinosaurs have been found already.

You have to look very carefully to spot fossils in rock. This may be easier in cliffsides or hills that have been worn away by time and weather. Paleontologists use picks, chisels, and hammers to dig out fossils. Soft brushes are useful for removing dust. Then they need to protect the fossil before it goes back to the lab. There, it needs to be separated from the rock and cleaned before being studied.

In many parks and other public land, it is illegal to dig up or remove dinosaur fossils. If you find one, take a picture and locate it on a map. Then report your find to the park ranger or local natural history museum. Some museums offer digging programs. Here are a few:

North Dakota Heritage Center

612 E Boulevard Avenue
Bismarck, North Dakota 58505

The North Dakota Geological Survey runs the dinosaur digs through the Heritage Center. You can sign up to join paleontologists at a real excavation site.

Wyoming Dinosaur Center

110 Carter Ranch Road
P.O. Box 351
Thermopolis, Wyoming 82443

If you find a bone at this center, you must register it there. The center keeps the fossil to study, but it records your name and where you found it.

Great Plains Dinosaur Museum

405 North 1st Avenue E.
Malta, Montana 59538

Children under 12 years old, accompanied by an adult, can join the Junior Paleo Field Experience. By going to a fossil site nearby, children learn about the science of dinosaur hunting and handle real fossils.

OTHER PLACES TO FIND DINOSAURS

Museums in Asia

China

Liaoning Paleontology Museum

Shenbai, Shenyang, Liaoning Province, 110136

The museum has a collection of over 10,000 fossils and reconstructions of dinosaurs found in Liaoning Province.

Zigong Dinosaur Museum

Da'an District, Zigong City, Sichuan Province, 643013

More than 200 dinosaur skeletons are preserved in this museum. The building protects the fossil bed to give visitors a view of the partially exposed bones.

Japan

Fukui Dinosaur Museum

51-11 Terao, Muroko-cho, Katsuyama, Fukui, 911-8601

The museum is only a few miles from the site of a rich dinosaur fossil bed. Many are now on exhibit in the museum, including over 40 dinosaur skeletons.

Museums in Australia

The Australian Museum

6 College Street, Sydney, New South Wales 2010

Animatronic dinosaurs greet visitors as part of the museum's large dinosaur exhibit. There is also a paleontology lab for kids to experience hands-on science.

The National Dinosaur Museum

Gold Creek Road and Barton Highway, Nicholls, Australian Capital Territory 2913

This museum contains the largest permanent collection of dinosaurs and other prehistoric fossils in Australia.

The South Australian Museum

North Terrace, Adelaide,
South Australia 5000
The museum's collection includes over
40,000 prehistoric specimens.

Museums in New Zealand

The Canterbury Museum

11 Rolleston Avenue, Christchurch
Central, Christchurch, 8013
The geology section includes a
mounted *Allosaurus* skeleton, as well
as the fossils of marine reptiles and
other prehistoric life.

Museums in the United States

Arizona

**The Arizona Museum of
Natural History**

53 N. Macdonald
Mesa, Arizona 85201
The museum's Dinosaur Hall includes
theropods, sauropods, and other
dinosaurs.

California

**Natural History Museum of
Los Angeles County**

900 W Exposition Boulevard
Los Angeles, California 90007
Dinosaur Hall contains a great selection
of skeletons and fossils. A visit to the
Dino Lab is a chance to see how the
exhibits are put together.

**University of California
Museum of Paleontology**

1101 Valley Life Sciences Building
Berkeley, California 94720
The museum has one of the largest
paleontology collections in the world.
It is mainly a research center, but it has
a vast database to search online. It hosts
an annual open day. Otherwise, there
are some exhibits, such as a mounted
Tyrannosaurus rex.

Colorado

Denver Museum of Nature & Science

2001 Colorado Boulevard
Denver, Colorado 80205
The exhibits here include re-creations of
ancient environments and a hands-on
fossil display.

Connecticut

Dinosaur State Park

400 West Street
Rocky Hill, Connecticut 06067
Walk in the footsteps of the dinosaurs at
one of the largest track sites in North
America.

**The Yale Peabody Museum
of Natural History**
170 Whitney Avenue
New Haven, Connecticut 06511-8902
The Great Hall of Dinosaurs features one
of the largest dinosaur murals in the
world, "The Age of Reptiles."

Georgia

**The Fernbank Museum of
Natural History**
767 Clifton Road NE
Atlanta, Georgia 30307
Explore the Giants of the Mesozoic
exhibit and find a massive
Giganotosaurus.

Illinois

**The Chicago Children's Museum
at Navy Pier**
700 East Grand Avenue
Chicago, Illinois 60611
Search for bones in a re-creation of a
wreal dinosaur dig.

The Discovery Center Museum
711 North Main Street
Rockford, Illinois 61103
Kids will love finding out about dinosaurs
and how scientists find them.

The Field Museum
1400 S. Lake Shore Drive
Chicago, Illinois 60605
This museum features Maximo, a
122-foot- (37-meter-) long titanosaur, as
well as Sue, one of the largest and most
complete *Tyrannosaurus rex* skeletons
ever found.

Indiana

**The Dinosphere at the Children's
Museum of Indianapolis**
3000 North Meridian Street
Indianapolis, Indiana 46208
There are fossil digs for the whole family.
Visitors can learn about the world of the
dinosaurs with other interactive exhibits.

Maine

The Maine Discovery Museum
74 Main Street
Bangor, Maine 04401
Learn all about fossil hunting, dig up
specimens, and more at the Dino Dig.

Massachusetts

The Museum of Science
1 Museum of Science Driveway
Boston, Massachusetts 02114
The museum features a large *Triceratops*

found in the Dakota badlands, as well as many other amazing fossils.

Michigan

The University of Michigan Museum of Natural History

1109 Geddes Avenue
Ann Arbor, Michigan 48109
Visitors can explore the many galleries and discover Michigan's largest collection of prehistoric fossils.

Minnesota

The Science Museum of Minnesota

120 W. Kellogg Boulevard
St. Paul, Minnesota 55102
Experience dinosaurs up close, and even put yourself inside the jaws of a *Tyrannosaurus rex*. The Paleontology Lab has hands-on fossil activities.

Montana

The Museum of the Rockies

600 West Kagy Boulevard
Bozeman, Montana 59717
The Dinosaurs Under the Big Sky exhibit in the Siebel Dinosaur Complex is one of the largest dinosaur displays in the world.

New Mexico

The New Mexico Museum of Natural History and Science

1801 Mountain Road NW
Albuquerque, New Mexico 87104
Visit here to learn about prehistoric life in Southwest United States.

New York

The American Museum of Natural History

Central Park West at 79th Street
New York, New York 10024
The Fossil and Dinosaur halls hold almost one million specimens.

North Carolina

North Carolina Museum of Natural Sciences

11 West Jones Street
Raleigh, North Carolina 27601
Visit here to find *Acrocanthosaurus* and *Thescalosaurus*.

Pennsylvania

The Carnegie Museum of Natural History

4400 Forbes Avenue
Pittsburgh, Pennsylvania 15213
Step back into the Age of the Dinosaurs

at the museum's Dinosaurs in Their Time exhibit to see dinosaur skeletons standing in fantastic, re-created habitats.

South Dakota
The Children's Museum of South Dakota
521 4th Street
Brookings, South Dakota 57006
Visit here to see dinosaurs in action. Two animatronic *Tyrannosaurus* dinosaurs are ready to say hello.

Tennessee
The Creative Discovery Museum
321 Chestnut Street
Chattanooga, Tennessee 37402
Kids can dig for their own dinosaur fossils at the Excavation Station.

Texas
The Houston Museum of Natural Science
5555 Hermann Park Drive
Houston, Texas 77030
The Hall of Paleontology houses more than 30 dinosaurs and other prehistoric creatures.

Utah
The Natural History Museum of Utah
301 Wakara Way
Salt Lake City, Utah 84108
The museum's collection includes over 30,000 prehistoric specimens.

Virginia
The Virginia Museum of Natural History
21 Starling Avenue
Martinsville, Virginia 24112
The Hall of Ancient Life includes a giant *Allosaurus*, and visitors can also take a peek at scientists at work in the paleontology labs.

Washington, D.C.
The Smithsonian National Museum of Natural History
10th Street & Constitution Ave NW
Washington, D.C. 20560
The incredible Hall of Paleontology holds dinosaur specimens as well as mammal fossils.

Wyoming
The Wyoming Dinosaur Center
110 Carter Ranch Road
Thermopolis, Wyoming 82443

This is a museum and a dinosaur digging site in one.

Museums in Canada
The Canadian Museum of Nature
240 McLeod Street
Ottawa, Ontario K2P 2R1
The Fossil Gallery is the place to see complete skeletons and take a walk through a re-created swamp forest.

The Royal Ontario Museum
100 Queen's Park
Toronto, Ontario M5S 2C6
Dinosaurs and other fossils from the Jurassic and Cretaceous periods are on display here.

Museums in Europe
United Kingdom
The Natural History Museum
Cromwell Road, London SW7 5BD
In addition to skeletons and an impressive fossil collection, the museum includes lifelike, reconstructed dinosaurs that move.

Oxford University Museum of Natural History
Parks Road, Oxford OX1 3PW

Iguanodon, *Cetiosaurus*, *Megalosaurus*, and many other dinosaur specimens are featured in the museum's fascinating collection.

Belgium
The Royal Belgian Institute of Natural Sciences
29 rue Vautier
1000 Brussels
This museum has the largest dinosaur gallery in Europe, with many skeletons on display. The paleoLAB is an interactive exhibit to dig for fossils and even rebuild a skeleton.

Germany
Natural History Museum
Invalidenstrasse 43
10115 Berlin
One of the museum's star attractions is *Brachiosaurus brancai*. It is 43.5 feet (13.27 meters) high and holds the Guinness Book of Records for the tallest mounted dinosaur skeleton.

READING FOCUS

Text Structure is all about the way a text is organized. When we know the structure, we can focus more of our energy and attention on comprehending what we read.

This book uses a Description Text Structure. It describes a topic and its characteristics using details, adjectives, and a logical order. Description texts often use examples to show and explain the main idea or topic.

Description texts usually include a lot of interesting details. We can use a graphic organizer to help us keep track of the most important information.

1. This is a Bubble Diagram, a strong graphic organizer for Description texts. Visit **www.worldbook.com/ resources** to download and print copies or create your own!

2. As you read and/or revisit the text, complete a Bubble Diagram for EACH section:
   • What Is a Dinosaur?
   • Shandong Tianyu Nature Museum
   • Dinosaur National Monument
   • Dinosaur Provincial Park
   • Digging Up Dinos

3. For each section, write the title in the center-most bubble. Next, add important details to the bubbles attached to that central, main idea. Remember, you do not have enough bubbles for *every* detail. Think critically to determine which details to include.

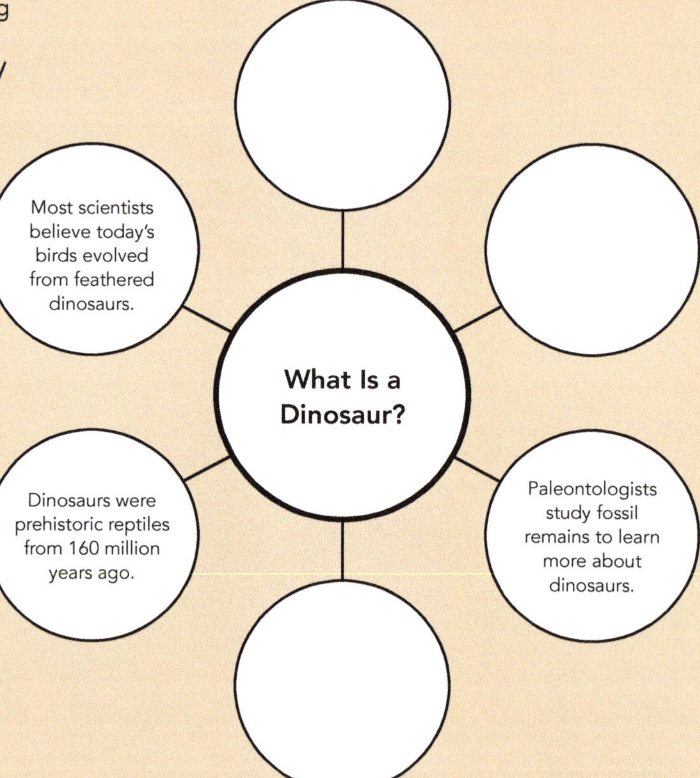

WRITING FOCUS

What do YOU think?

In your opinion, which of the four spotlighted locations would be best for finding a dinosaur?

Review the notes you took on your Bubble Diagrams. Use evidence from the text, supported by logical reasoning, to answer the question. Your writing should include:

- A **hook** where you grab your readers' attention
- A **thesis statement** where you state your opinion
- At least 3 **reasons** why that is your opinion
- At least 3 **details** that support each reason

Use an Opinion Writing Graphic Organizer to sort through your thoughts before you write your response. Create your own or download and print a version from **www.worldbook.com/resources.**

Opinion Writing Graphic Organizer

Hook and Thesis:	Reason #1	Detail #1
		Detail #2
		Detail #3
	Reason #2	Detail #1
		Detail #2
		Detail #3
	Reason #3	Detail #1
		Detail #2
		Detail #3

You might have noticed some words in this book written in *italics*. That means they are vocabulary terms! **Challenge yourself!** Can you include at least 5 of these words in your opinion writing?

INDEX

ACKNOWLEDGMENTS

Cover: © metha1819, Shutterstock
TP: © Herschel Hoffmeyer, Shutterstock
6–7 © Orla, Shutterstock; Maksim Shchur, Shutterstock
8–9 © Ton Bangkeaw, Shutterstock
10–11 © Dotted Yeti, Shutterstock; Rodos Studio, Shutterstock
12–13 © Gorodenkoff, Shutterstock
14–15 © Bruce McAdam, Wikimedia Commons
16–17 © Catmando, Shutterstock
18–19 © Michael Rosskothen, Shutterstock; Bruce McAdam, Wikimedia Commons
20–21 © Michael Rosskothen, Shutterstock; Natursports, Shutterstock
22–23 © Nina B, Shutterstock; IrinaK, Shutterstock
24–25 © Jacob Boomsma, Shutterstock; Herschel Hoffmeyer, Shutterstock
26–27 © vagabond54, Shutterstock; Stephen Saks Photography, Alamy
28–29 © Warpaint, Shutterstock; Marco Semprevivo, Alamy
30–31 © John Elk III, Alamy
32–33 © Steve Boer, Shutterstock; Daniel Eskridge, Shutterstock
34–35 © Nick Fox, Shutterstock
36–37 © Gorodenkoff, Shutterstock
38 © Konstantin Zaykov, Shutterstock
40–45 © Stephen Shaver, Alamy